BUTTERFL.

Foreword

How do we discover the true nature of God? I have spent much of my life seeking to explain the reality of God and the relationship that we can have with Him. But no number of sermons or teaching sessions can speak to us as deeply and sincerely as a real-life story.

It's when we hear a true story of the way in which God has touched one heart, one life, with His power, that our 'academic' knowledge becomes real. It's then that we meet with a living God, who has the power to transform us and draw us into a new way of living. This is such a story.

I first met Crystal in 2019, shortly after the events she describes in her story had come to an end. We both arrived in the church where I was the pastor at about the same time. Crystal was a young lady with a very real love for Jesus and she was on fire with a desire to serve God. What I didn't know, until she gave me a copy of the manuscript for this book, was the story of how she came to faith. It is a deep, personal and moving account, which speaks of the power of God, and the new life that He offers to us. Crystal is brave enough to share her story with the world.

Through this story, we discover how God is at work – how God can take the life of one person, and transform her, through the power of His Spirit.

As you read this story, be open to learn about God – how He is at work in the lives of people today. But do more than just learn – be open to the possibility that God will work in your life, to bring transformation and the 'fullness of life' that our Lord Jesus speaks of.

God took Crystal and turned her into a new creation. He can do that for you!

Tim Eady

Preface

God had a plan for my life. God created me and birthed me into my family for a reason and specific purpose. My family is not the ideal family. We are not the trophy family, and we were not born with a gold spoon in our mouths. The family that I was born into has multiple generational issues. My family has a history of Incest, Mental Health, and Financial struggles.

I was born on the gorgeous islands of Trinidad and Tobago. I was three years old when I flew from Trinidad and Tobago to Jamaica with my mother and younger sister. Jamaica was where our family was—my father, grandparents, etc.

Growing up in Jamaica was difficult. It was difficult because I lacked stability, safety, soundness, and a firm foundation. My parents were both unemployed. My mother was a victim of domestic violence, and my father was a drug addict and a gambler.

My home was unstable because I would see my father on weekends and spend the weekdays with my grandmother or mother. From a young child, I had thoughts of suicide. I attempted suicide by putting a knife on my wrist. I attempted suicide by putting a wire around my throat. I attempted suicide by wanting to walk out into a moving bus or jumping out of a driving car.

When I found the Lord, I knew I had a strong foundation in Him. He is my Rock. Jesus is my firm foundation, and I know that I can count on Him. He will never leave me nor forsake me! Furthermore, he will never leave you nor forsake you.

Introduction

T his is my testimony. It is 100% real, authentic, and raw. This testimony is about my life and what God has done and continues to do. I write my testimony in a book to share with you. I want you to experience the love of Jesus and get to know Him. I was the "woman at the well," I was the "woman with the issue of blood," I am that woman to whom God proclaimed loosed and forgiven of sin, with the instruction to go and sin no more.

I am the woman who received the Father's love in her heart. I am a woman who wants to share her struggles, transformations, hardships, and pitfalls. Still, most importantly, I want to share my journey with you – my journey as the *butterfly woman*. The butterfly woman is any woman who have had to endure hard times, walk through patience, stand still in prolonged suffering, and yet is made to be better and more robust - I am *that* woman. I share my testimony because I want you to be confident in who you are. I found the confidence I need from within and not in external things. I want you to be a part of my life as my sister and friend. We are all in this together, to the end and into eternity. Thank you for picking up this book; I truly hope you enjoy it!

Contents

Chapter

1

Humble Beginnings I

"L ook, Look!" Saiyra D exclaimed, "It's you! It even has the same colours you are wearing!" The butterfly fluttered its unique orange, white and black wings flying across our picnic area at Himley Park. We gathered near the lake in the summer of 2017 on a clear, crisp and sunny day.

The group shared sweets and flavoured fizzy drinks, and we ate lots of Indian Samosas. I had lots of friends in the church. We always go on trips, have parties, and celebrate birthdays and achievements. We prayed together and for each other. We cried together and belly laughed with each other. Nevertheless, life has not always been sweet. Life has not always been butterflies and was not always good. Let me give you a backdrop.

I grew up in Lionel Town, Clarendon, on the island of Jamaica. Lionel Town is a small village where everyone knows everyone. There are lots of shops, bars, and supermarkets. There are many fruit trees in people's yards and wild animals everywhere. Growing up in Lionel Town has helped me to be fearless. The people's characters range from tramps to beggars to insanity to drug addicts and gunmen. You name it, and it is there.

My mother, grandmother, and other relatives raised me in a Jehovah's Witness home. I was so uninspired; I did not enjoy Kingdom Hall. The service commenced with a weekly routine; they sang hymns, read the Word from the Watchtower and discussed relevant topics. To me, it was pretty mundane, too staged, and too obtuse.

On occasions, we visited Pentecostal churches. In the Pentecostal church, people wore their Sunday best. They wore fancy hats with feathers hanging off, matching suits for the gents and beautiful shades of matching lipsticks for the ladies. The ladies wore high heels and they would make sounds as it hit the gravelled road. Each step would be hurried as they walked briskly to be at church to take part in the praise and worship.

In the Pentecostal church, people expressed themselves freely as they fell over, kicked their shoes off, and shook. I never understood then that it was the anointing of the Lord on those people.

We were poor, and my parents could not afford to send us to school. We did not have clothes, shoes, enough food, and so forth. Our basic needs were unmet, and we moved around a lot of the time. I attended a Christian Preschool, Hope Basic School. I never understood it, but God surely knows how to work miracles, and He works mysteriously. God visited my teacher in a dream and told her to allow me to attend the rest of the school term for free. With financial support, I graduated from preschool and went on to primary school. God continued to provide for me to stay in school and get a good education.

People said that nothing good would come from me. The stigma around my family's mental health issues and economic status allowed people to speak negatively about my life. Consequently, my home life had much to do with what people said. We had very little to live off, and we struggled. We all slept in one bed, all four of us in a one-bedroom house in a single-parent home.

I know the pressure of being unable to provide for us had taken the better of my mommy. I felt like she regretted having us as children. She would say things like, 'I wish you came out as blood' or 'I wish I never had any of you.' 'I swear on my life; I wish you were never born.' My mother exclaimed this while holding onto her breast and looking at the sky. You get the picture. That was my foundation.

Contradictory, my mommy is the strongest woman I know. She raised eight children on her own and had a miscarriage on top of all of that. *Mommy, I know life has not been the kindest to you. Furthermore, given the circumstances, I know you did your best.*

Having children or getting married was not in my peripheral view as a dream growing up. That is because nothing good was expected from me, so I did not expect anything good for myself.

"Nathanael said to him, 'Can anything good come out of Nazareth?' Phillip said to him; "come and see" (John 1:46 NKJV).

Jesus was also brought up in a small town, the Son of a teenager named Mary. When Jesus was under scrutiny, they said nothing good came out of Nazareth, and they were implicating that Jesus was unlikely to succeed at anything. But yet, He advanced as our Saviour. Listen, there is hope for you and I. There is hope because it does not matter what sort of unorthodox home you came from. Jesus, too, came from an unorthodox home.

I understand the dynamics of today's society, and I know that bad things happen or will happen to us all. And this is why I am writing this book. The butterfly had to be a caterpillar, and the caterpillar had to metamorphose and struggle in its cocoon. What are you struggling with? Is your cocoon child abuse? Is your cocoon trauma? Is your cocoon an addiction? Is your cocoon having depression? Is your cocoon….Whatever your cocoon is, you can break through, my friend.

My cocoon: I was left alone and vulnerable. As I shared, my family has a history of incest, and I became a victim. Unfortunately, at a tender age, all that was on my mind was to get intimate because I was introduced to perversion at a young age. I had witnessed my parents *doing it* with their lovers and they were not discreet about it around me. I think I wanted to share some same level of closeness with someone.

I needed a hug occasionally and wanted to cuddle with my parents. I longed for an emotional connection with them. I longed for affection from my caregivers. And sadly, because I was exposed to lovemaking, I became inquisitive and curious. My little brain interpreted my longing for love and attention as needing physical intimacy. This pattern would continue until I encountered Christ.

Chapter

2

Humble Beginnings II

Unfortunately, I was only eight when I first had a sexual encounter. Maya Angelou had a similar experience; she was abused at eight. Maya Angelou went mute for years after her abuser was murdered. I never told anyone about my abuser, and even if I did, it would not have made any difference. I quickly learned to keep my mouth shut about 'shameful' things. My caretakers would say, 'what happens in our home stays in our home.' Therefore, I had the right to remain silent. According to my folks, staying quiet was normal and the best thing.

If I mentioned to my guardians that I was molested by an older man, I would get in trouble. So much so that when I was molested;

even though I never told mom, she knew somehow. I was wet with his smelly sperm on my clothes. She sat me in a chair in the bedroom, and she beat me.

Despite the lack of protection and safe space, I desired a normal childhood. My siblings were my saving grace. We lived in a one-bedroom house, so we grew closer every day. We always played together, listened to music, and danced for fun. We helped each other with our homework. We sat and did puzzles together and would play out in the garden. We shared sweets and made each other laugh. I remember we had competitions about who was the funniest. We counted and noted the number of jokes told in a day, and the person with the most jokes won. We also had our own reggae concerts and dancing competitions. I was not a good dancer! We pretended to be Destiny's Child, a famous group in the 1990s. It was the best of times and the worst of times.

We loved having juicy beef patties as a treat. I loved watermelon, too, as a treat. On weekends when mom could afford to go to *May Pen* Market, she bought us juicy beef patties and watermelons! Once in a blue moon, we had new school shoes and a pair of slippers. The school shoes were for school, and the slippers were to be worn everywhere else. We walked around bare feet if we had to. One time, I wore my slippers out but came home without them. Mom threw a rock at me, it landed on my hip and bruised me. She then ordered me to go and fetch them. That was how sacred having a pair of sandals was.

Our school uniform was for school, and the clothes with holes and rips were to be worn everywhere else. Sometimes, I would wear my aunt's clothes with some Bobby pins holding them up at the waist. Bath time was in a basin, and we would share bath water. Our hair was washed and combed twice monthly. Mom looked after our hair with Jamaican *Purelene egg and protein* shampoo/conditioner and treated it with Aloe vera or Jamaican Tuna plants, a.k.a Cactus.

Mom was keen on personal hygiene. We had to brush our teeth every morning without fail, scrub behind our ears, clean the sole of our feet, and wash every part of our bodies. When we ran out of toothpaste, we would use cooking salt or African chew sticks to brush our teeth. Breakfast was crackers with milo or herb tea, and the herbs were picked out of the garden. For dinner, we had fried dumplings with tin mackerel or stew chicken back with white rice.

We did not have a cooker. We used a coal stove to prepare meals. We did not have a refrigerator either to cool our drinks or store leftovers. We could not afford a loaf of bread, so we bought half or a quarter from the shops. Same with meat. We purchased meat weighing up to a pound or two pounds instead of a whole chicken. Some Sundays, we grated coconut for our rice and peas dinner.

When we were at Granny's, we had breakfast, lunch, and dinner without fail. Granny was a nurse at Lionel Town Hospital, and when she retired, she could provide the necessities using her pension. Also, she had support from her Jehovah's Witness friends. When things were challenging, and Mom could not find the money for food, she took out her anger on us. It was during those times that we planned an escape route. We felt as if she would kill us, so we planned our safety net whenever she got angry. My siblings and I would run away for refuge at Granny's house.

Exhortation for struggling mommas:

I was not nurtured and cared for as a child. I cannot change what happened in the past, but I sure can change what will happen in the future.

"I can do all things through Christ who strengthens me." (**Philippians 4:13 NKJV**)

You, too can do anything; you can raise your children with self-worth and be a single mom, a divorcee, or a rape victim. You can submit the next generation to be full of zeal for life. Again, if you are a single mom, you can raise your child/ren in a good home. I would advise you to reach out and ask for help. Please do not say things to your children out of anger, fear, or worry. Your children will live what they learn. Train your child to value themselves, treat them with respect and love, and cuddle them.

"Train up a child in the way he should go, And when he is old he will not depart from it." (**Proverbs 22:6 NKJV**)

Listen to your children whenever they are speaking so they can tell you things that are hard to talk about. Be sure to cultivate a safe space for them to be themselves. Do not call them names that they are not. Ask for help; no one will judge you for doing the right thing. And take one step at a time…if you are overwhelmed, it is okay, take a breath and keep going.

You are important. Look after yourself. If your child is a product of a broken home, you can still raise your child to be thankful. Children only need you to be there for them, and if you are showing that you are doing your best, rest assured that you are good enough. God will honour your sacrifice. Do not worry if your children are rebelling or doing things you do not like. They can find their way back. Keep praying for them, or start to pray if you are not already doing so.

Prayer for your Children

Dear Lord Jesus, thank you for my children and family. Please cover and protect them. Watch their going out and coming in. Please, Lord, hide them under Your wings. Cover their gifts, talents and destiny from the enemy. Help me Lord, to love and be there for them. When things get hard, give me the strength to carry on. Renew my mind into becoming the parent you want me to be. In your loving name, I pray, Amen.

Chapter

3

Loss of Innocence

I was an obedient child; anything my parents asked me to do, I would do it. I was not an unruly child, and I was very servant - hearted for the most part. I looked up to my parents and wanted to please them with every fibre of my being. I was the sibling who tried to solve my parents' worries. My parents suffered from mental health issues, and their way of dealing with the stress was to turn to drugs. In their state, they did not have the capacity to teach me that I was fearfully and wonderfully made. **(Psalms 139:14 NKJV).**

My parents could not teach me how to stay safe in the streets or say no to paedophiles. They just did not have the conviction to protect me because of their mental illness. I never saw my parents forming or cultivating relationships with a significant other. My father had women coming to the house, spending the night, and then a new face the next day, and it was so all of the time. Sometimes, I was in the same bed beside my father while he would *have his way* with these women. From a young age, my idea of a relationship was obscured because I thought it was okay to have intercourse with multiple partners.

When I started to desire to have a relationship, I did not know how to start, how to get to know someone or, better yet, how to be faithful. So, when men groomed me, I had zero regard for saying no. It was too late; I could not unlearn what I knew about relationships. I do not think my parents realised the imprint that their serial dating had on me, and I followed the blueprint. I gave up my virginity to a man I barely knew. I never knew his surname, his address, or if he had siblings or parents. Our conversations were: 'Do you want to meet up after school or on the weekend?' I had zero credible role models in my life; I did not value myself because I simply did not know how to.

Unfortunately, I believed my purpose and value came from befriending men. When in reality, my identity as a Child of God was muddled with a false sense of belongingness and worthiness outside of God's will. My happy place was not at home; it was in the arms of strange men.

I am from a single-parent home, as my dad immigrated to the United Kingdom (U.K) when I was thirteen years old. I had to survive somehow - I relied on men for one; a sense of purpose, and two; to take care of me financially because it was hard in a single-parent home. It did not matter that I was seeing three men at a time - I perceived all the attention to gaining a sense of belongingness, and I thought I found my haven. I was happy, and even though I never felt moved by having intercourse with them, I enjoyed their company very much. I felt taken care of because I was now a pro in getting what I wanted. I had the latest mobile phones and money, and I was going out to parties. I was at parties and clubs, smoking drugs, and drinking alcohol. I was going from pillar to post without any accountability.

My carefree behaviour got me expelled

from one of the top schools in Jamaica - Garvey Maceo High School. I got expelled for a build-up of things, but the main thing was smoking weed in the girls' toilet. I was a terrible teenager and thought the world was mine for taking. Do I think I was a thug- that smoking was cool? *Wrong. It was not. Getting high is not cool.*

I was about 14 years old when I almost lost my life. I recall, one night, coming home from a night out, and to my surprise, I was being watched. It was dark, and I was about to enter my room. I suddenly blocked out while standing on my veranda to open the door. He did something to me, and I was hurt. I did not comprehend what had happened, but he was drinking, and I woke up in a pool of blood. My friend who lived next door was present with me.

It was all a blur as I was troubled with internal questions; how did that happen? Why didn't I feel anything? When did I get off the veranda and on the ground? Did I roll? How did the beer bottle break? Now that I was on the floor, in a pool of blood, I had to be taken to the hospital. As I got to the hospital, I found out that I needed to have some stitches. I got hit with a beer bottle, and it broke on my left upper shoulder. I was attacked in the dark.

Of course, I knew who it was. Nevertheless, I was not about to tell the nurse because she would have wanted me to get the police involved. You see, I got attacked from behind by my jealous sugar daddy. He was an angry, jealous drunk who questioned my whereabouts and would often track my every move. I never knew when he was following me, but he stalked me at school, at home, when I was out, etc.

One evening, after school, I was talking to my friends. When I reached the school gate to hop in a taxi to go home, I saw his big white van parked outside my school. I jumped into his van, and he punched me in the face before I could say anything. I had blood gushing out of my face, all over my pink and white uniform. He drove me home. He said he saw me chatting with a man and got jealous. I got home and buried my bloody uniform. But you see, my perpetrator, was feeding me, clothing me, and caring for the family with his money, so getting rid of him was hard. He left me with scars even today.

Consequently, because of these incidents

I flew to England, where my father was, to escape. I never did saw my perpetrator again. I could have been a dead victim. My drunk sugar daddy could have killed me out of rage, jealousy, or anger. The Lord protected me because many girls in violent relationships like mine do not make it out alive.

"But you, O Lord, are a shield for me, My glory and the One who lifts my head. I cried to the Lord with my voice, And He heard me from His holy hill. Selah, I lay down and slept; I awoke, for the Lord sustained me" (Psalms 3:3-5 NKJV)

The Lord sustained me and gave me a new start. On 23 December 2004, I flew on British Airways to join my father in the U.K. We had not seen each other in over three years and I was nervous about meeting him at Manchester, U.K airport. I was nervous because we were meeting face to face, and I worried about seeing his reaction to one; I got an expulsion and two; I was beaten up and three; I had to flee the country. He wanted me to be a lawyer, so I knew he was disappointed.

When he picked me up from the airport, he took my suitcase but never hugged me. My father commented on my weight, saying I looked skinny, and then handed me a can of nourishment to drink. To be real, my heart sank into my chest with disappointment. I felt gutted. At least, I thought he would hug and welcome me to England. I only uttered a few words during the car journey from Manchester to Birmingham. I felt that there was nothing to say after he embarrassed me.

The next morning, I woke up, and it was the same cold reception I received from him. My dad and other relatives were downstairs in the kitchen, rampaging through my luggage to get things I bought from Jamaica. But no one stopped to hug or welcome me to the country. However, the United Kingdom was my new home, and I had to embrace whatever would happen. Not long before I realised I was in a new country, but the abuse followed. Read on.

Chapter

4

A new start or not?

I missed my sisters; we were the 3C'S (our girl group name!) We have been through thick and thin together. A hole was created in my heart because my norm would be very different in a new country. I was right; everything was different. For instance, I did not see any boarded-up houses like the one I lived in with my siblings. I saw no hustlers on the streets trying to sell you anything! I never saw stray dogs, skinny cows, or greedy goats roaming the streets. I saw flocks of pigeons - and that was as wild as it got!

England houses are all brick and adjacent, with many detached and semi-detached houses. I also noticed that public transport has a buzzer on its buses to press when stopping. The first time I went on a bus, I shouted, 'one stop, driva!' Then my companion told me that pressing the buzzer works better next time.

Christmas was spent indoors with a feast of turkey, spuds, pigs in blanket, stuffing, cranberry sauce, apple sauce and brussel sprouts. As it was cold, everyone wore socks and snuggled under a blanket on the sofa with a big, bright Christmas tree full of wrapped presents underneath.

The winter mornings were absolutely cold and frosty; each time I exhaled, my breath turned to vapour. I shivered with chills up my spine, especially when waiting for buses at the bus stop. I tried rubbing my hands together to get "warmish."

When I saw the snow for the first time, I stooped down and touched it with my bare hands to feel the crunch, and it was freezing cold. I loved the U.K.'s winter fashion: the fancy scarfs, high knee boots, lovely padded jackets, gloves - what's not to love?

Even though I was in love with winter fashion, I also, in the same breath, missed the Caribbean. I missed the loud music belting out of speakers echoing in the streets, the smell of curried goat, and the rum cake aroma that perfumed the neighbourhood. I missed the grand market on Christmas Eve in May Pen with my crew and a Heineken in my hand. I missed seeing the rude boys with a spliff hanging off their mouth corners. I missed going to my friends' houses and eating many mangoes, almonds, guineps, and june plums. I missed the street corner dominoes and ludo game playing. I missed my 'freedom' and I could not find a way to break out of being homesick and step into something new.

I lived in Birmingham with my father and a few other relatives. I was in a house with a washing machine, a cooker that comes on with a click, a lovely upstairs bathroom with hot and cold water taps, and a television with hundreds of channels to watch.

At first, I could barely understand the thick British accent, and it sounded like they were not speaking English. The more I was around the British accent, the easier it was for me to understand. My father's accent was still *patois*. He is a proud Jamaican that takes pride in his heritage and culture. However, he caught a bit of the 'brummie' accent because I would laugh at him every time he said something 'brummie'. We kept the tradition of having rice and peas on Sundays and playing reggae music when cleaning the house.

I noticed the young girls were of bigger bodies than I had. Whenever they told me their age, I gasped with disbelief that we were the same age or age group. I was sixteen, skinny with long legs, arms, curly hair, and darker skin. They looked like older women, and they could not believe my age either. Again, I felt like a fish out of water with my Jamaican accent and skinny legs and zero things in common with them. Nevertheless, I was not about to return to Jamaica, so I might as well pull my socks up and get on with it.

My father was working as a cleaner. He did not make much money doing that, as it was only for a couple of hours a day. He also was in a lot of debt. Bailiffs knocked on the door most weekends, but he hid from them.

I never envisioned my life in the U.K. to be *rosey,* but I also did not expect my father to treat me the way he did and the trials I would endure. At sixteen years old, my father was supposed to be my provider. He refused to provide and told me to practise prostitution with his friend for money. I was an obedient child; every week, I went to his friend's - he was an older man that lived about a 10-minute walk away. Then dad took some of the money I was given for himself, and in addition I had to contribute to bills and grocery shopping.

Life started to feel lonely again, and I reverted to cigarettes, marijuana, and alcohol as a distraction from my pain. The pain of isolation, internal loneliness, and infirmity. The pain of my father using me for money.

My mindset was very poor. I could not think for myself or even have an opinion. I was frequently told to *shut up* or get scolded for "talking back." I felt growing up, like I had to be obedient and do whatever was asked of me. I had no backbone whatsoever - I was enslaved.

However, at that age, I knew love was missing in my life, and I was on a quest to find it. I was still looking to my dad for reassurance, affirmation and love, but it never came. He did not respect me, enslaved me, brainwashed me and frankly made me feel bad about myself.

I knew how he wanted me to accumulate good grades in school. He was always so disappointed with me when my grades were not up to mark. I remember when I was in grade three of Watsonton primary school, and I was doing some maths problems for homework. My dad was helping me with my sums and long divisions. I could not get the gist of the sums.

My father scolded me until I could solve my maths homework. I was crying tears and counting my fingers at the same time. The next day, I was called to the front of the classroom to solve the equation on the black - board. I got it correct, and the class cheered me on! My father was focused on me getting good grades, not understanding that he was neglecting my value, my self - worth and the protection I should have received as a child. I felt unloved by him.

Love is patient and kind, and I was on a mission to find someone- anyone who was willing to be kind-hearted and patient to me. I was looking for love in persons but soon realised that their love was impure; they loved me only when I could please or satisfy them or behaved in ways they approved. So, it is safe to say I was conned and wool was over my eyes. That wool came off when I opened the Bible and read about love, particularly the scripture below. I was opened - mouth gob - smacked by the adjectives that broke down what true love was! To me, this was it. This was everything!

"**Love is patient and kind; love does not envy or boast; it is not arrogant or rude. It does not insist on its own way; it is not irritable or resentful; it does not rejoice at wrongdoing but rejoices with the truth. Love bears all things, believes all things, hopes all things, and endures all things. Love never ends." (1 Corinthians 13: 4 - 8).**

Chapter

5

Where is the Love?

The first time I found out that I fell pregnant was when I visited my local sexual health clinic to check if I had any sexually transmitted diseases. I finally got around to getting checked and having my blood tested. I remember the nurse asking me if I wanted to do a pregnancy test, and me being completely oblivious that I was pregnant, said yes. In a few minutes, she told me I had a positive pregnancy test. I was not expecting that.

In hindsight, I did not love myself, so loving and caring for a baby was not on my radar, so I immediately thought about an abortion. When I put it to the child's father, he agreed for me to go to the clinic and have an abortion. I kept that I was pregnant a secret.

In fact, I had kept three pregnancies a secret. I know the scrutiny that would have followed had I told my dad I was expecting a baby.

The second pregnancy came as a shock too. The same thought again was to abort the baby. I went under anesthetics again, and when I woke up, the process was over. However, the process of forgiving myself was never easy. I cried so many tears after realising what I had done. Because, in my mind's eye, I was a bad girl. I felt terrible about myself. I relived the negative words of my parents and caretakers. They rang in my ears louder than Big Ben's bell.

When I was having my third abortion, the nurse I consulted said that, 'because this is your third abortion in the space of two years, if you go ahead with it you might never have children again.' Even with the nurse's reasoning, I did it anyway. I was adamant not to bring a child into my world of hopelessness, brokenness and restlessness.

You are not your pain.

If you had an abortion, or three like me or maybe more. Or, in the same way, if you have done something you are ashamed about and not proud of, like fornication, addiction to porn or masturbation - you are not a bad person. God loves you so much, and He sees your pain.

"For God so loved the world that He gave His only begotten Son, that whoever believes in Him should not perish but have everlasting life." (John 3:16 NKJV)

God cries when you cry. He carries you even when you do not feel held; He is there with you. He has forgiven you, my dear, and you do not need to be ashamed. You are redeemed by His precious blood over your life. Your life does not end because you made a mistake - or maybe it was not a mistake. Perhaps you had the abortion/s or [your wrongdoing] with your mind made up. Consciously, you decided to go ahead and do it. Let me encourage you; you are still the apple of His eye.

"Keep me as the apple of Your eye; Hide me under the shadow of Your wings." (Psalms 17:8 NKJV)

There is nothing under the sun that is

new to God. He is a big God-He can handle the big stuff. Do not believe the lies that will condemn you. You are free from condemnation.

"There is therefore now no condemnation to those who are in Christ Jesus, who do not walk according to the flesh, but according to the Spirit." (Romans 8:1 NKJV)

God is not expecting perfection from you, but He wants to give you a life of hope, a future, and an expected end. God has a plan for your life, and do not forget that. He is patient and kind, and He is in love with you.

In hindsight, I was looking for love all my life, and I could not find it in all the showers of gifts, money and going out to the best parties. I was an 'empty well.'

Chapter

6

Daddy, don't do that

"Do you love me?" he asked cunningly. "Of course I do," I replied hesitantly. Convincingly, he then said, "Gimme a kiss." I was looking for other words, but nothing came out of my mouth. We were both standing face to face in my small bedroom. I saw my Bible behind his shoulders on the shelf and suddenly felt God's Spirit. The fear of my dad left me instantly, and all I had was compassion for him. I looked into my father's droopy eyes with compassion, but before I knew it, he gently lowered me to the bed and went on top of me. In the morning, I had just woken up, and nobody was present to protect me.

I remember when Jesus was on the Cross, He had compassion for those who were persecuting Him - He said:

"Father, forgive them, for they do not know what they do." (Luke 23:34 NKJV)

I pushed myself up so that he could get off me and went downstairs to the kitchen to make a cup of tea. My father followed me to the kitchen. He was in pursuit of getting that kiss and much more. Whilst in the kitchen, he started to plan where we must meet so that he could *have his way* with me.

He offered me money to let him perform sexual acts on me. He asked if I could remember how sexually active I was in Jamaica. At that moment, I felt like he was saying to me: 'Oi, *you are a harlot, and I want to have my way with you. You are used to this, so why can't I have you now?*'

I was standing in the kitchen, mixing the sugar in my tea, and I also noticed that I had the company of kitchen knives around me. I had a glance at my life in my head. I was about to stab my father in his heart to kill him. I took hold of the knife, ready to charge at him, but I did not see prison when my whole life flashed before me. I thought of another op-

33

tion, a simpler option. A choice that would not land me in jail for the rest of my life. I stabbed him in the leg and ran outside in my sleepwear to escape.

A few days passed without seeing him, and then, in the thick of the night, there was a knock on the door. I ran downstairs to open it, and to my surprise, it was my father standing at the door. He said 'a you mi come fah yuh nuh." I thought I was in a movie. It reminded me of that scene in *Dancehall Queen (a 1997 Jamaican Movie)* when the bad guy - Priest, came to kill Sunny. In that scene, Sunny was playing dominoes under the street light when Priest approached them. Sunny got up to defend Marcia, his friend, as Priest was there to make trouble. That was when Priest walked up to Sunny and whispered those words in his ear. "A you mi cum fah." Then Priest pierced a knife into Sunny's stomach and killed him on the spot.

My father put me on the spot when he reminded me of my miserable childhood. Right there, he took my dignity, worth, and self-esteem. He disregarded me as his daughter. His eyes were deceiving him from our father-daughter relationship. He saw me as one of his concubines.

In Chapter 1, I spoke about my "cocoon." I referred to the caterpillar's way of breaking out of its chrysalis. I mentioned my vulnerability and how I was taken advantage of, unfortunately. You see, the butterfly takes a couple of days to break out of its cocoon. In the same way, it will take us a while to break out of dysfunction. Especially if you have lived it.

My father was AIDS/HIV positive at the time he wanted sexual favours. I found out about this when I had a phone call from relatives to come back home to look at him. He lay stiff in bed, refusing to eat or drink or go to the hospital. When I got there and saw him, he was skin and bone. I asked if he was okay, and I called 999 for an ambulance. The ambulance was there in less than three minutes.

When we got to the hospital, they found my dad a room. We were alone in the room when he called me to come closer next to his bed. *Was he about to pull another one of his stunts?* He told me, "I have HIV; please don't tell anyone."

I was my father's 'sacrificial lamb' per se.

He told me that he had joined a cult to gain wealth; houses, cars, money, jewellery etc. The leaders of his cultist group advised him to sacrifice the person he loved the most. I thought he was losing his mind when he started talking about the cult he had joined. He wore a ring on his finger given to him by them.

When I listened to him talking, it sounded like he was convinced about everything he said. The cult world was real to him, but I thought that he was having hallucinations because he told us he got a big house and a jeep.

I visited him in the hospital almost every day. He was in a secluded room because of AIDS/HIV, and the hospital was being cautious. I visited with fruits, food, beverages and token coins so he could watch TV in his hospital bed. I was there for him throughout his recovery. I held his hand when he was walking because he was wobbly on his feet. I pushed him in his wheelchair when he got discharged from the hospital with his medications.

Even though I knew his intentions were not good towards me, I was there for him and prayed for him with the church members.

Repeat this if you are from a dysfunc -

tional background or experience of some level of dysfunctionality: I *do not have to mirror traits of dysfunctionality. Even though I may experience it from time to time, I can do better by choosing to forgive and move on. Dysfunctionality does not define my actions because I can make a difference and I choose to forgive and move on. In Jesus' name. Amen.*

Do you remember in **1 Corinthians 13**; it says that Love...is patient and kind...not easily angered, it keeps no records of wrong doings. Love...protects? Do any of Paul's words, (the writer of what Love is in 1 Corinthians 13,) ring truthful with my mother and father? No. It does not but I was able to put myself in Paul's shoes to grasp the concept of Love. God was showing me how important Love was and still is, so I dived into this scripture and personalised it by replacing *Love* with *Crystal*. So, *Crystal is kind and patient and so on.* I was starting to love myself and God started revealing how much He loved me!

"When my father and my mother forsake me, Then the LORD will take care of me. Teach me Your way, O LORD, And lead me in a smooth path, because of my enemies. Do not deliver me the will of my advers -

aries; For false witnesses have risen against me, And such as breathe out violence." (Psalms 27:10-14 NKJV).

As Christians, we live in the realm of the Spirit. We can allow God's word to work in us; to heal, vindicate and make us victors. On top of that, I urge you to talk to an expert or someone you can trust. Take it from me, you do not want to keep secrets and bottled-up emotions. Bottled-up emotions will manifest in ugly ways. Expose the enemy; speak out and get the help you need to overcome.

I was taught from a young age to keep quiet about shameful things and to keep secrets. I was not encouraged to speak up or get the police involved when need be. As a result, my emotions and feelings were disorganised and I made silly mistakes. My interpretation of situations was different from the norm. Frankly, I was an adult but had the mindset of a seven year old. I was so naive, shallow and empty on the inside. All types of people had access to me because my home life mirrored that. All sorts of people walked in and out of our homes. People that were alcoholics, drug addicts and those that preyed on the innocent. They all came to chill and talk about all sorts of nonsense amongst themselves; nothing edifying. And that was normal for me.

Chapter

7

A change has come

It was in the cool of a lovely cloudy day, and my friend and I were walking to Asda Supermarket to buy some groceries. We were going to make dinner and we needed a few items. When we got to Asda, we noticed a small church adjacent, so my friend said, "let's go in." The door was open. When we got in, there were two men inside; a black man and a white man. (The black man; I still keep in touch with him until this day. He is a very influential person in his community.) I think they were just about to wrap up to go home. They hospitably sat us down, offered us water then proceeded to enquire about our spontaneous visit. We told them the reason for popping into Asda supermarket. Nonetheless, I was led to the Lord with a prayer of salvation and was given a Bible.

This was the same Bible that was in my room mentioned in Chapter 6. The black man helped me pray out loud the prayer of Salvation. I uttered the prayer word for word with my hands clasped, head bowed and eyes shut. I knew how to do these gestures when praying because I saw it when I was a child.

My friend was talking to the white man about how torn she had been feeling inside. He offered her some sound encouragement from the Bible. Then we thanked them and went on our way.

The Prayer of Salvation:

"Dear Lord, thank you for your Son Jesus Christ and what He did on the Cross for me. Thank you for dying on the Cross for my sins. I know that I am a sinner. Please forgive me. Come into my life and change me, In Jesus' name we pray. AMEN!"

This was and still will be the **_BEST_** deci -

sion I have made in my life. I gave my life to Jesus. I remembered that I did not hesitate to pray - God called me and I answered immediately. God did not need to send a whale to swallow me before I listened. I knew right there and then - I felt it on the inside while praying that I was doing the right thing.

I went to church the next Sunday and the following Sundays after that. I soon got the feeling that I belonged. I felt the warmth of being around people who all have a common vision. That vision is serving God practically as much as they could. A church sister offered me some lovely dresses so that I can wear them to church. The dresses were beautiful and modest, a far cry from my ripped jeans and hugging figured vests.

I felt a knowing in my heart that I was going to be okay. I looked forward to going to church every weekend. I have never felt so certain about anything- that I wanted to be around people who were kind hearted, loving and joyous. More than anything, however, I wanted to hear sermons about Jesus. God was calling me to surrender my life and have a relationship with Him. He was also calling me to a faith - filled family.

"So then faith comes by hearing, and hearing by the word of God." (Romans 10:17 NKJV)

The Lord was probably calling me from a little girl but I could not hear Him because the enemy used sin to block my channel to God. The intimacy, the sense of belongingness and purpose that I desired, was what I needed in Christ. But the enemy dumbfounded me and alluded to abused me. The enemy gave me a false sense of identity, tricked me with money and a false sense of security. The enemy did everything to bring me down and rendered me powerless. I was putty in his hands. I was serving the enemy with my body and mind and it can only be the resurrection power and blood of the living God that could redeem me.

God called me into his family and I was no longer a candidate for Satan. A church friend took me into their family home. *It was game time*. I was about to destroy every plan of the enemy against my life. I went to every prayer meeting, Sunday meeting, conference and crusades.

Instead of smoking drugs I was now getting high on the Word of God. I was getting high on scriptures, particularly The Gospel;

Matthew, Mark, Luke and John. I read the Bible as if I was digging for *gold.* I quit smoking cigarettes and marijuana, stopped going to parties and even stopped listening to secular music. I mean, I would not have been able to tell you the latest song or biggest hit. I started practising celibacy. I plugged into a church and listened to worship songs until I felt like the melodies were a part of me... I felt at home in God's love.

Bob Gass (1944 - 2019) wrote hundreds of daily devotions titled *'UCB Word for today.'* His words of wisdom always gleamed off its pages and struck a chord in my heart. At home' in God's love' by Bob Gass below:

'Make yourselves at home in my love.' John 15:9 The Message (MSG).

When someone says, 'make yourself at home' it means you're welcomed and accepted. And that's what Jesus means when He says, 'make yourself at home in my love.' You never have been and will never be loved by anyone as much as God. The reason why you may have such a hard time grasping that concept is that you have nothing to compare His love to.

Nothing could make God love you more than He does right now and nothing could make Him love you less.

The great irony is that we spend our lives trying to earn His love when it can only be received by faith. In his gospel, John says; 'What marvellous love the Father has extended to us!' Just look at it! If we believe we're called Children of God that's who we really are.

But that's also why the world doesn't recognise us or take us seriously because it has no idea who Jesus is or what He is up to. (1 John 3:1-2 MSG). You may have grown up with parents who withheld their love or who weren't capable of expressing it. God doesn't do that. Throughout scripture, He keeps saying, 'I love you. I love you. I love you!' C.S Lewis wrote 'God created us to be the objects of His love! Sometimes our actions make us unlovely, but we're never unloved. And because God loves us we have value. And nobody can take that value away.

God's love revealed at Calvary fastens itself onto flawed creatures like us, and for reasons none of us can ever quite figure out, make us precious and valued beyond calcula -

tion. This is love beyond reason. And this is love with which God loves us.'

Chapter

8

Down by the river

I realised that my personality was that of a chameleon. I am a product of my environment. Now, I am saved and born again, I succumbed to the Christian culture. I was born again into the family of Jesus'. This means that I understood the fight and warfare between the two Kingdoms. The Kingdom of God versus the Kingdom of Darkness. I knew we are all spiritual beings and that we wrestle not against flesh and blood.

"For we do not wrestle against flesh and blood, but against principalities, against powers, against the rulers of the darkness of this age, against spiritual hosts of wickedness in the heavenly places."

(Ephesians 6: 12 NKJV)

For example, I was an addict. But I was using that as a crutch because I needed to feel strong. I was weak, an easy target and did not know wrong from right. The family of God assured me that Jesus was my Rock and so I could drop my crutches and stand on Him. I was also very lonely and sought attention from the menaces in society. But again, I was affirmed of how Jesus will never leave me nor forsake me. I was not alone - He was right there. I clung to His Word. His Words, to me, were like fresh water gushing down the reservoir of my life.

I started to metamorphose in Christ; I was starting to accumulate wings to fly above worthlessness, low self-esteem and lack of identity. My name is Crystal and it means a precious stone. Crystal shines beautifully when the light hits it. Jesus is that light. I am NOT an *idiot*, *stupid*, or a *harlot*. I am <u>precious</u> and <u>valuable</u>.

"And he showed me a pure river of water of life, clear as crystal, proceeding from the throne of God and of the Lamb."

(Revelation 22:1)

My confidence was slowly emerging from the junction of my heart and I was moving forward. And even though I was the same Crystal; tall and skinny on the outside but I was the daughter of the King and loved.

Since being in the church, I have had two engagements but we never made the altar. I think I was rushing ahead of God plus I was convinced that the man who first approached me in the church would be my life partner. Well, that did not go according to the "*Crystal's chronicles.*" I still did not know how to do relationships. God was using circumstances to teach me what a healthy relationship would look like for me.

I saw that the girls in church were so desperate to behold a husband. Remember I told you that I am like a chameleon - my intention too became about beholding a husband. I went through a season of obsession about finding my life partner to the point that for every single, good-looking guy my eyes spotted in church, I would quickly whisper a prayer to God - asking 'Is that him, Lord?'

Unfortunately, I became like the Isreal -

tes; physically I went back into slavery and bondage, mentally I went back to my old ways. I was doing the same old things and was expecting different results.

Even though I was a backslider, I held on to my faith and believed in Jesus Christ. The Lord never stopped loving me but my foundation needed to be stronger, rooted in Christ. In order, when the storms of life come I know where to go for shelter.

"I am the Lord, and I will bring you out from under the yoke of the Egyptians. I will free you from being slaves to them, and I will redeem you with an outstretched arm and with mighty acts of judgement. I will take you as my own people, and I will be your God. Then you will know that I am the Lord your God, who brought you out from under the yoke of the Egyptians. And I will bring you to the land I swore with uplifted hand to give to Abraham, to Isaac and to Jacob. I will give it to you as a possession. I am the Lord" (Exodus 6:6-8 NIV)

God is so faithful and He sees us. He knows what we need. This is not a cliche - He actually got our best interest at heart.

Remember, He is our good Father and when we ask Him for anything He will give us what we need.

"Do not fear, little flock, for it is your Father's good pleasure to give you the kingdom." (Luke 12:32 NKJV)

I am reminded of a sermon a guest speaker delivered at church. He said "not everyone will get married; some of you are not called to get married." He then carried on to say, "what if that's you, what if God doesn't want you to marry? Can you live with that?" It was food for thought but I did not want to digest this. I was thinking that that message was not for me.

I was looking to get married and settle down to honour God's plan for my life. I believed that I was ready and I was in the waiting room - to get next in line. I have seen everybody else with engagement announcements and lavished receptions, and I was wondering if it would ever be my turn!

A sister invited me to a Bible study. It was unlike any Bible study I have been to before. And so, I went week after week and from there my roots grew deeper in Christ. The group dissected witchcraft, unforgiveness, cult, generational curses, fears, incest, personal history, family history, identity crisis and a lot more. I went through Christian therapy every week for about a year.

I learned about the breaking of chains; the chains of witchcraft, incest etc and how to break every single stronghold. I went through the whole list with a fine tooth comb with my spiritual mothers. We went over every aspect of my life to dig up all the unfruitful roots that were bearing bad fruits in my life. The Psalmist puts it perfectly when he says:

"I have pursued my enemies and overtaken them; Neither did I turn back again till they were destroyed. I have wounded them, So that they could not rise; They have fallen under my feet. For You have armed me with strength for the battle; You have subdued under me those who rose up against me. You have also given me the necks of my enemies, So that I destroyed those who hated me." (Psalms 18:37-40 NKJV)

And then we began planting good seeds; reciting all the truths about who I am in Christ.

The truth shall set you free, my friend, the truth about Him and how your life is of much worth. You were born with worth. From the very moment you were born, you had worth in you. Yes, from the moment you were born; and you took your first breath, Heaven rejoiced and Angels were dispatched for you - to keep you in all your ways.

Chapter

9

Planted by the River

I am grounded in God and everything He has done for me. He set me free, washed me, cleaned and resurrected my life. I was going down a dark tunnel without light at the end of it. Until a man named Jesus whispered "I love you" in my ear then I started to turn away from darkness to light.

When I understood that that light could not be outshined or distinguished, I was empowered to walk in my God-given right as a Child of God. God started to bless me and favour me. He lavished me with a three-week holiday in Jamaica. He sent me there to see my family. It was wonderful. I saw, prayed, and played with my nieces, cousins, nephews and siblings.

Then, the Lord started putting it on my

heart that I would have a family of my own. I knew that God would bless me with my heart's desires in His timing. The desire was so powerful, I had to press into it, with God. Sometimes, I would place my hand on my stomach and pray to God to bless my womb. I know I had three abortions, so I prayed to God to bless my womb so I could have children. It was spoken over me that my last abortion would result in infertility but we serve a God of second chances. Amen.

I used that potent desire that I had and prayed with that same unction until it was released. Every time that desire came back strongly in my heart, I surrendered to God to bless my womb with babies.

The thought of being a mom hijacked me that I would sometimes break down with tears in the children's section of department stores. I called my spiritual mother, and I went to her in tears, and that is when she went and interceded for me. She prayed ruthless prayers on my behalf until my heart was not troubled. And whenever I went to stores and would stumble upon the baby's or children's aisle, I was at peace.

For you, it is important to have somebody that can pray, a prayer warrior who knows how to battle in warfare, just like in the 'War Room' movie. And you, too, must start praying in the spirit to get your breakthrough. Remember that God wants to bless you with your heart's desire for marriage or children or something else.

When I met my husband, I did not know immediately that he would be my husband. The funny thing is I remembered when God spoke to me and said, 'Your husband is waiting for you on Temple Street.' *And no, I did not run to Temple Street there and then to look for him!* When the Lord spoke those words, I was courting my ex. One evening, we were going to a Jamaican restaurant for dinner, and he went inside to place our orders, and I stayed in the car, and that was when I heard from the Lord. To be honest, I was courting my ex with plans for marriage, and we were participating in marriage counselling etc. So, I never did regard the thought as from God. Fast forward years later, that relationship crashed like a train wreck. God gave me 2 Corinthians 5:17 to meditate on during my healing.

"Therefore if any man be in Christ, he is a new creature: old things are passed away;

behold, all things become new." (2 Corinthians 5:17 KJV)

But lo, behold, I met my husband for the first time on Temple Street. My husband was single for about five years before we met. He told me after we got married that he was waiting for love.

Throughout my life, I have never received a perfect gift other than the gifts God gave me. The gift of love, the gift of caring, the gift of being supportive, the gift of strength, the gift of compassion, the gift of courage, the gift of kindness, the gift of bravery, the gift of faith, the gift of freedom in Him, the gift of a new life.

God favoured me with a husband that loves me. This love makes me want to be a better person every day. I love him enough to respect him. I am hands on heart committed wholeheartedly to my husband. He is so patient, caring, kind and gentle. My husband is a man after God's own heart.

We visited the most beautiful cathedrals and churches while courting and shared mesmerising long walks along the countryside. We loved being peaceful. We went to museums restaurants, and shopping together but visited churches and cathedrals most. We took Bible studies and Bible courses and prayed together. That man has got the gift of the prophetic. We have a sound support system and people who will help us in our walk. My husband is the epitome of love. He truly loves me, all of me. I can be myself around him - and I love that.

I believe his love for me mirrors how Christ loves His bride - the church. Christ does not run away from His bride due to flaws. His love is relentless, and this is how my husband loves me. And when God connects you with your spouse they will see beyond the flaws and shortcomings because your spouse will look at you with the eyes of pure and sacrificial love. The love that never ends. They will look at you through the lens of Christ.

God knew that the characteristics of my husband would be what I needed. For example, he is a good father, and his love for his family is admirable. He is hardworking, caring and faithful.

However, I have been through hard times with close family members, and my trust in people has been tainted. And so, I do not allow my circumstances to dictate my outcomes in life. I rely on God to give me a fresh perspective and a sound mind.

I am reminded of the three Hebrew boys in Daniel 3, in the fiery furnace who instead chose to hold unto God, believing their faithful God would rescue them.

My life mirrors the three Hebrew boys because of the fiery furnace. I was not in an actual fire per se, but in the struggles I have been through, God was there with me. Now, I refuse to bow down to people's opinions of me or the limits they had placed on me.

God says ALL things are possible and that I am who He says I am. *I am favoured. I am loved. I am free from condemnation. I am blessed. I am forgiven.* And the list goes on.

"For God did not give us a spirit of timidity *or* cowardice *or* fear, but [He has given us a spirit] of power and of love and of sound judgement *and* personal discipline [abilities that result in a calm, well-balanced mind and self-control]." (2 Timothy 1:7 AMP)

Chapter

10

Sweet Melodies

My husband is a blessing to me; frankly, he aided in my recovery. Whenever we went on our long, peaceful walks along the picturesque countryside, we would hold hands and embrace the authenticity that comes with nature. One day, he ran out in the middle of the field to pick me the only red flower that stood out in the fresh green pastures. He hurried back with the single, red flower jumping over the high grasses in the fields. I chuckled. Then he said, 'here, this is for you.' I put the flower up to my nose and smelt the petals. Then I tucked the flower in my hair and took a selfie.

I know what to expect of him; he would go out of his way to make me feel seen. Furthermore, he will always hold my hand through the walk of life. When we were about to welcome our daughter into the world, we were in the birthing room, and he offered his hand for me to squeeze through my contractions. He never let go, even though I gripped his hands through the pushing and birthing of our little gift.

Our daughter's birth was spontaneous. She was keen to meet us! We laboured with her for about three hours, and then she was here. The Lord revealed to us what we should name her and provided everything she needed. It was a supernatural birth lasting only three hours - from the first contraction to retrieving the placenta. The Lord prepared me for this birth and told me to push when it was time because I was very anxious. I was nervous and thinking about how I will give birth. We did what the Lord told us to do, and He was faithful. There she was, as precious as pearls, and all wrapped up nicely in her white towel while we took photos for memory.

I felt a surreal calm about being her mommy because she, too, was a calm baby and only cried whenever she was hungry. I held her close and looked into her big beautiful, brown eyes and my heart sparkled with love and my stomach fluttered with butterflies. She was worth the struggles of 'yesterday.'

My husband and I were super proud of her, and we intentionally discussed her upbringing. We discussed giving our daughter the best start in life; by this, I mean we will love her unconditionally.

We will ensure that she knows what love is and her home will always be a haven. We do not strive to give her toys to compensate for spending time with her. We buy her toys to play with, but we will always have our arms wide open for her to return to. I prioritise my life with her in mind like; for instance, I was earning a good wage at my job, but the hours were unsociable, and I would barely have time for her. I was missing her first words and first steps, so we decided that I would stay at home.

Then we were pregnant with our second baby! And it was yet another supernatural birth. Again, he came out very quickly. My husband said, "It's like your body was designed to give birth." He was so astonished by my courage and how I handled the rapid contractions without pain relief. From the first contraction to the birthing of the placenta, it was under three hours. My husband knew that the first birth was quick, so when I woke him up in the night to drive me in the car to the hospital - he woke up straight away, or else we knew the baby would have been a home birth! Our baby boy is so joyful, and he laughs with glee! His face just oozes joyfulness.

I'm grateful to be restored from my losses per se. My family is my ministry. God gave me the ministry to show up every day with the God-given grace available to me afresh. I show up with the knowledge of the Power of the Holy Spirit living on the inside of me. There is nothing too hard of a challenge that I cannot overcome. There was a season when God prompted me to believe He could give us bigger and better things for our children's upbringing.

"In so much that thy former things were little, and that thy last things be multiplied greatly. (in so much that though thy first things were few, but thy last things shall be greatly multiplied.)" (Job 8:7 WYC)

My husband and I received compliments about our children all of the time. Whenever we would go out to public affairs, somebody would always walk up to us, tap us on the shoulder and let us know that we have 'Angelic' and beautiful children. My daughter's nursery too, gives us compliments about how confident and sociable she is. We are accustomed to having people telling us about the great job we are doing.

But we give God the Glory for the compliments because it is only by His Grace. We believe the Lord looks after our children, too, not just us.

Our children are well-behaved in churches, supermarkets, road trips, and even events that might be mundane to them. They do not crave attention when we are outside. We are grateful for this and know it is by His Grace. At home, we established them by lavishing our time on them. We set boundaries, too, because they can not have chocolate or ice cream for breakfast! We interact with them on their level, singing all the nursery rhymes and then singing them again and again! Playing peek-a-boo even when she is hiding in plain sight! We let her get involved in tasks like helping to feed the dog her food. She loads the washing machine and tidies up her toys after she is done with them. I am reminded of the scripture that tells us:

"And we know [with great confidence] that God [who is deeply concerned about us] causes all things to work together [as a plan] for good for those who love God, to those who are called according to His plan and purpose." (Romans 8:28 AMP)

My former days versus my latter days are opposites because what I know now I did not know then. God has done a great work in me and has taught me everything I know now. God taught me to be a mom and a wife and love others. Those attributes were not things I had ever seen growing up. But I am glad about God's renewal of my mind, restoration and redemption.

God is not a respecter of persons, the same restoration is awaiting you.

A self-care letter for you:

Dear you,

Hallelujah! Glory be to God! He is worthy to be praised! Yes, go ahead and give Him all the Glory! He alone deserves the highest praise. He deserves your dance, your shout, your heart's cry.

This is how we fight our battles. We fight our battles in worship and praise and adoration for King Jesus. You have victory on the inside of you; you have overcome. You have worth. You are a winner. Do not let the strains of this world silence you. I know you get busy with chores, work and life. Do not let the hustle and bustle stop you from giving God your adoration. You can fracture the Lord in your mundane daily routine. You can put God first, despite your calendar being full.

You know, there is a scripture that tells us that we must acknowledge God first then He will organise our life in the way it should. You should understand God sees your schedule and your tomorrow before you can. Do not lose heart. Do not throw in the towel. It will get hard and feel like life is too much. But good times are just around the corner.

There is nowhere that you can go where God is not there with you and that should be liberating to you.

Your relationship with the Lord will determine how much fight you have in you.
When the good times come and your season is flourishing, still put Him first. When you get your breakthrough, you get a new job, a new car, you have found a spouse, you signed that contract, you got healed etc.
Still fracture the Lord in your happy moments. Even if it is 'thank you, Lord, thank you.' Then go on ahead and enjoy yourself. Saying a heartfelt thank you to the Lord is like bumping fists or doing a high five, or doing a secret handshake with God.

Love,
Crystal xx

Notes

Notes

Notes

Facebook @ Crystal Silverwood

Instagram @ Crystal.flourish